# What's under the bed?

**Mick Manning and Brita Granström**

# W
## FRANKLIN WATTS
LONDON • SYDNEY

What's under the bed?

Floorboards are under there,
floorboards and dust.

bedbug

House dust is a mixture of fluff, hair and dead skin. Tiny creatures feed on dust. They are too small to see, but if you looked at one through a microscope it would look like this. → mite

# What's under the bed and the floorboards?

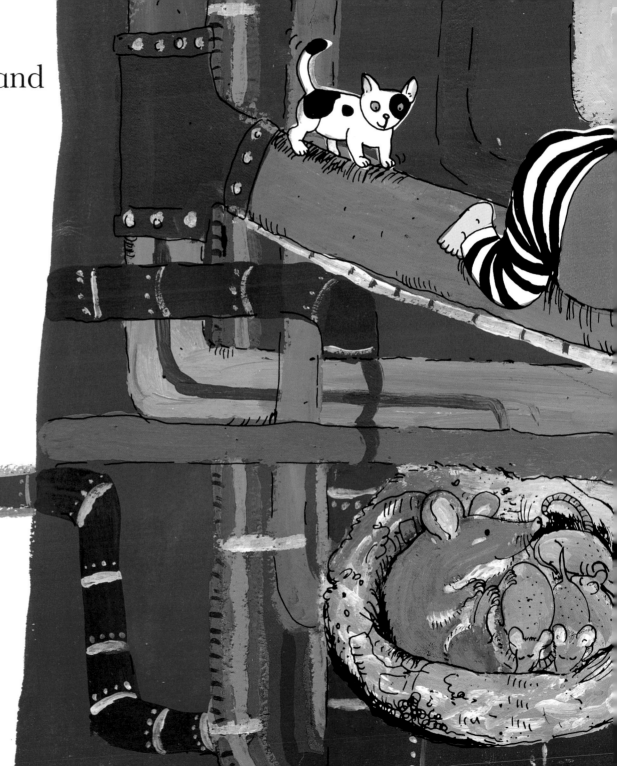

Wires and pipes go under the floor and behind walls. They carry electric power, gas and water into and around the house. Waste pipes take away waste from the toilet and kitchen.

4

Some water pipes are wrapped up to insulate them...

Insulation keeps the water in the pipes warm.

Wires and pipes are under there. Electric wires, and warm water pipes where a mouse has made her nest.

What's under the bed, the floorboards, the wires and pipes and the mouse nest?

A tree has about as many roots underground as it has branches above ground. Plant roots grow into the soil to find their food and water.

Soil is made up of tiny bits of rock mixed with air, water and rotted leaves...

Soil is home for many small creatures.

centipede

earthworm

beetle grub

Soil is under there, soil and plant roots where worms and minibeasts live.

What's under the bed, the floorboards, the wires and pipes, the mouse nest, the soil and the roots?

Queen - who lays all the eggs.

Workers - are females - who do all the work in the colony - finding food and looking after the colony's eggs and babies.

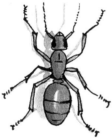

Drones - are males that only live long enough to help the queen lay her eggs.

Ants make homes underground and dig long tunnels with sleeping places, babyrooms and rubbish dumps.

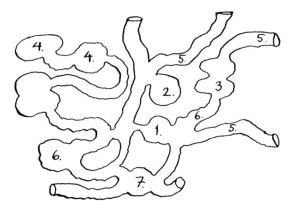

1. Queen with eggs
2. Queen with larvae
3. Pupae
4. Ants hatching
5. Workers gathering food
6. Pupae and larvae being moved by workers
7. Rubbish dump

Ants are under there, a colony of busy ants.

9

What's under the bed, the floorboards, the wires and pipes, the mouse nest, the soil, the roots and the colony of ants?

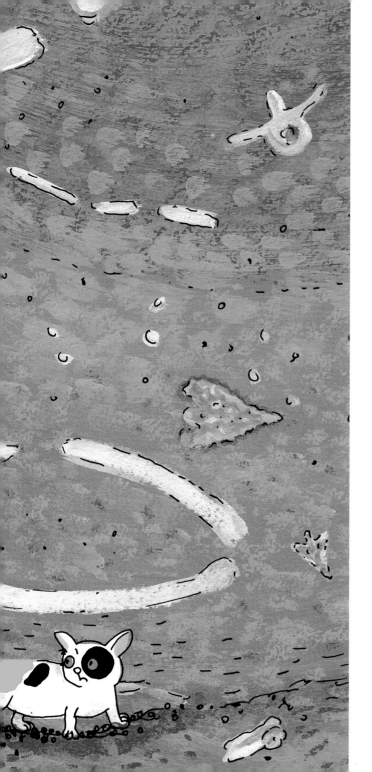

Clay - is actually a sort of rock, it is soft, wet and sticky.

Clay hardens when heated in a kiln (a special oven) to make pottery.

an old kiln

People dig clay out of the ground to make plates, cups and saucers and many other things.

a modern kiln

Clay is under there, clay hiding bones and arrowheads left by people from long ago.

What's under the bed,
the floorboards, the
wires and pipes, the
mouse nest, the soil,
the roots, the colony
of ants and the clay?

Many cities in the world have saved space by building railways that carry passengers deep under ground. Long moving stairs go from the surface to the platforms.

A tunnel is under there. A dark, noisy tunnel where underground trains thunder by.

What's under the bed, the floorboards, the wires and pipes, the mouse nest, the soil, the roots, the colony of ants, the clay and the noisy tunnel?

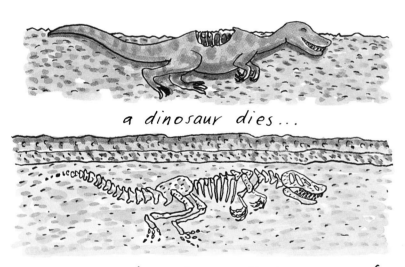

a dinosaur dies...

over millions of years it becomes a fossil.

Fossils are the hard remains of dead prehistoric animals or plants. Squashed together with gravel and sand they become stone.

You might find a fossil yourself if you look in stones and pebbles.

A dinosaur is
under there,
a dinosaur fossil
buried between
layers of stone.

What's under the bed, the floorboards, the wires and pipes, the mouse nest, the soil, the roots, the colony of ants, the clay, the noisy tunnel and the dinosaur fossil?

Prehistoric people living thousands of years ago often lived in caves. They painted pictures on the walls of the animals they hunted...

Stalactite

Stalagmite

Pointy stones on the roof and floor of the cave are made by water dripping and leaving tiny bits of stone behind. They are called stalactites and stalagmites.

Caves are formed when soft stone is worn away by underground rivers.

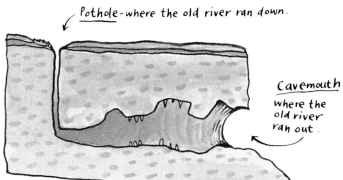

Pothole - where the old river ran down.

Cavemouth where the old river ran out.

When the river dries up it leaves a cave.

A secret cave is under there, a cave with prehistoric paintings on the walls.

What's under the bed,
the floorboards, the
wires and pipes, the
mouse nest, the soil,
the roots, the colony of
ants, the clay, the
noisy tunnel, the
dinosaur fossil and the
secret cave?

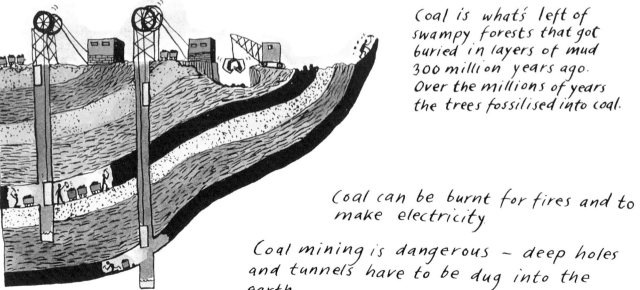

Coal is what's left of
swampy forests that got
buried in layers of mud
300 million years ago.
Over the millions of years
the trees fossilised into coal.

Coal can be burnt for fires and to
make electricity.

Coal mining is dangerous — deep holes
and tunnels have to be dug into the
earth.

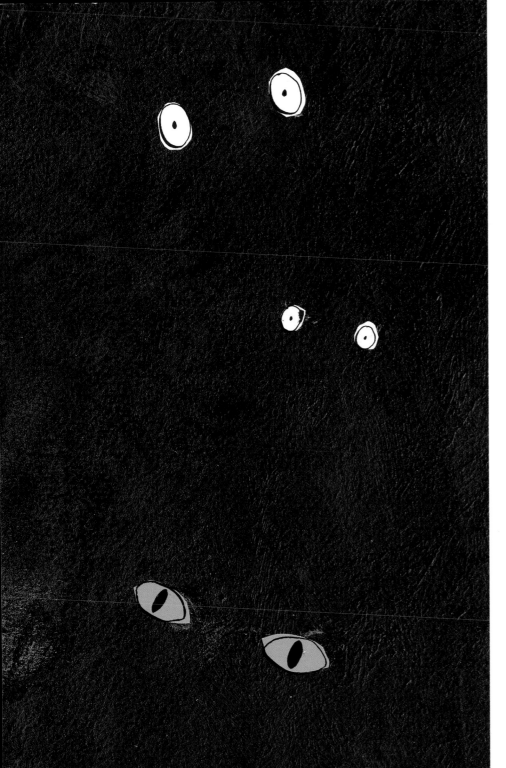

About 100 years ago pit ponies were used to pull coal trucks. Even small children were sent down the mines to work.

Miners wear helmets to protect their heads.

A coal mine is under there, an old coal mine, where rusty machines lie in the dark and fern fossils can be found.

What's under the bed, the floorboards, the wires and pipes, the mouse nest, the soil, the roots, the colony of ants, the clay, the noisy tunnel, the dinosaur fossil, the secret cave and the coal mine?

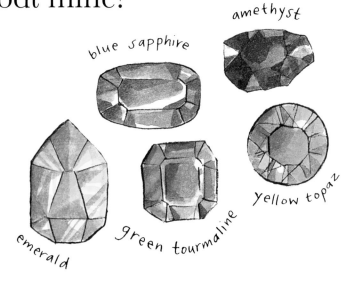

blue sapphire

amethyst

emerald

green tourmaline

yellow topaz

Deep underground hard rock can become so hot it melts. Sometimes gold, silver and crystals are left behind when this happens.

Gold and precious crystals are dug out of the ground in mines and are cut into special shapes to become "jewels."

gold

green zircon

silver

diamonds

ruby

Crystals and precious metals are under there. Quartz and emeralds sparkle among silver and gold.

What's under the bed,
the floorboards, the
wires and pipes, the
mouse nest, the soil,
the roots, the colony of
ants, the clay, the
noisy tunnel, the
dinosaur fossil, the
secret cave, the coal
mine, the crystals and
precious metals?

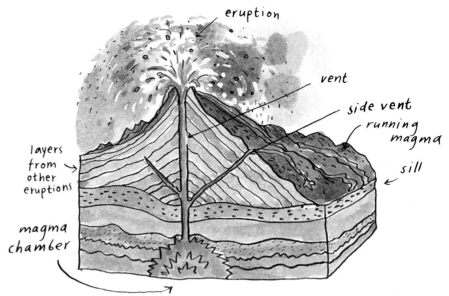

eruption

vent

side vent
running
magma

sill

layers
from
other
eruptions

magma
chamber

Magma is a sea of melted rock 700 kilometres deep. No one has ever drilled a hole this deep!

But we know about magma because it forces its way to the surface sometimes, through cracks in the Earth's surface - this is what we call a volcano.

Magma is under there, molten rock hotter than boiling jam. Imagine a heat so fierce it melts rock.

What's under the bed, the floorboards, the wires and pipes, the mouse nest, the soil, the roots, the colony of ants, the clay, the noisy tunnel, the dinosaur fossil, the secret cave, the coal mine, the crystals and precious metals and the magma?

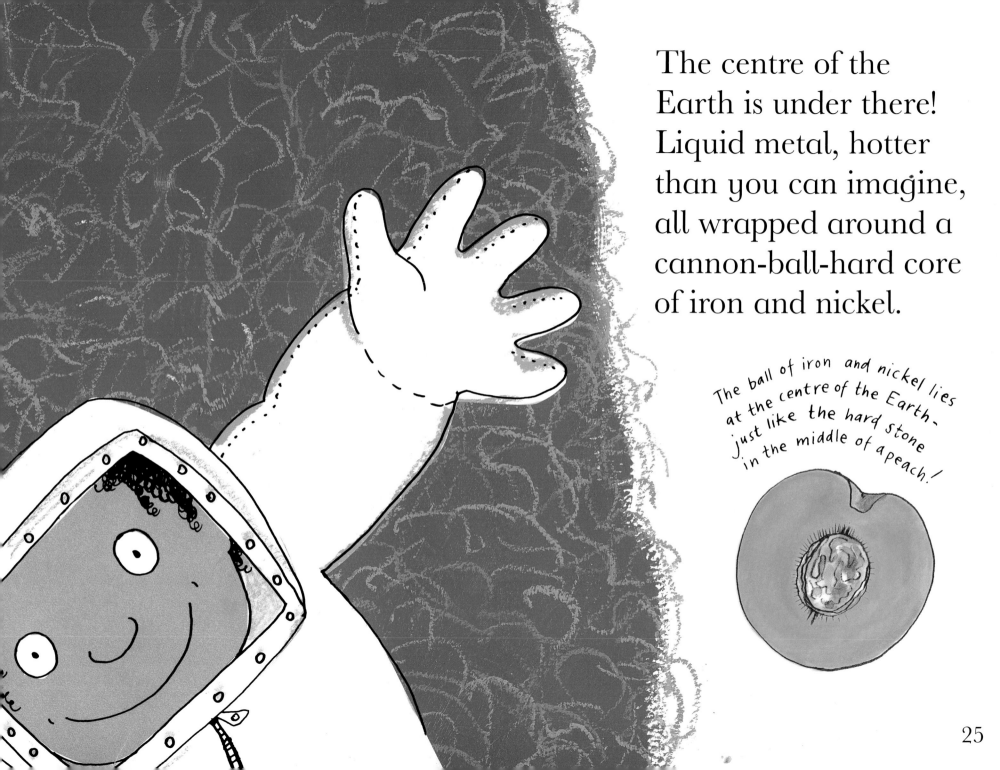

The centre of the Earth is under there! Liquid metal, hotter than you can imagine, all wrapped around a cannon-ball-hard core of iron and nickel.

The ball of iron and nickel lies at the centre of the Earth – just like the hard stone in the middle of a peach!

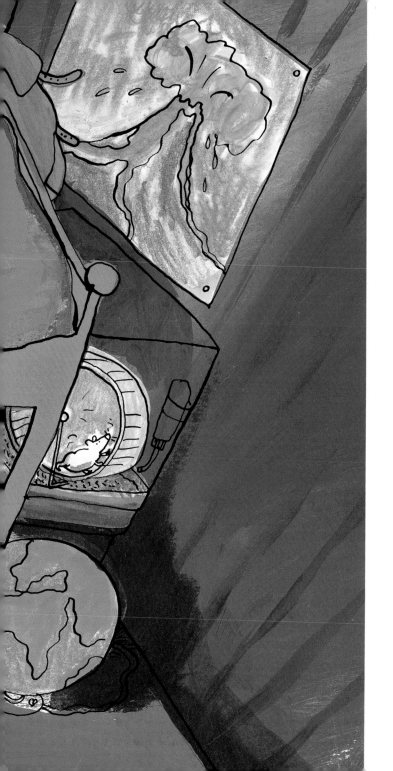

So ...
the centre of the Earth,
magma, precious metals
and crystals, a coal mine,
a secret cave, a dinosaur fossil,
a noisy tunnel, clay,
an ant colony, roots, soil,
a mouse nest, pipes and
wires and floorboards

....... are what's under the bed!

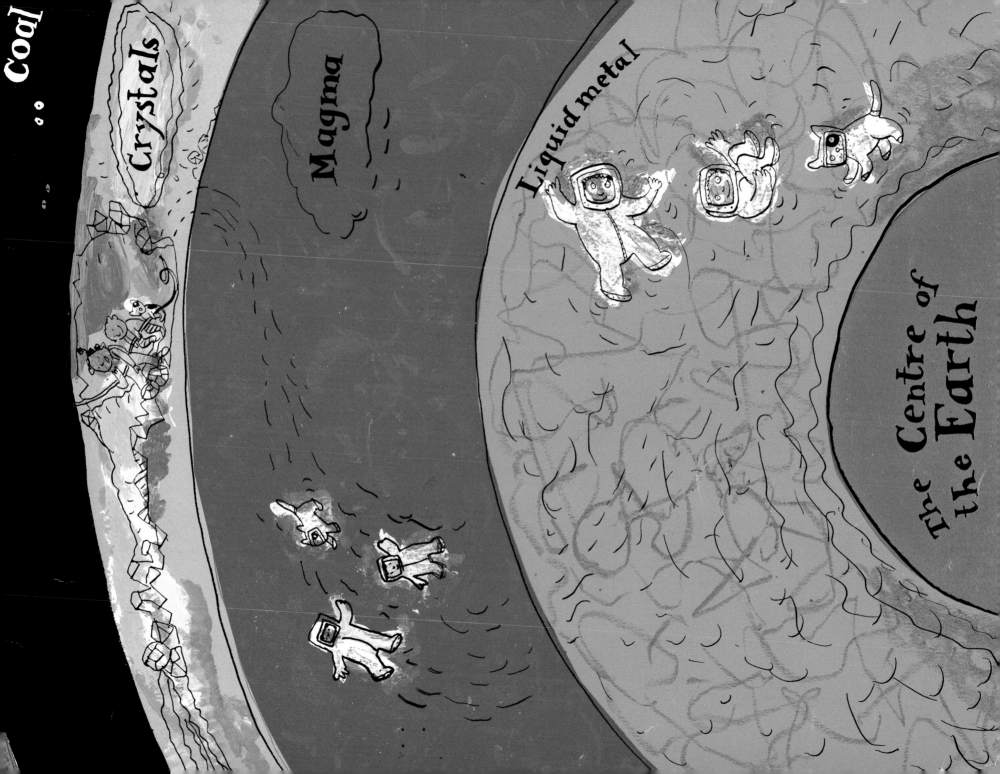

# Helpful Words

**Colony** a group of animals all living and working together (page 9).

**Dinosaurs** prehistoric reptiles that lived on Earth until about 65 Million years ago (page 15).

**Fossil** the remains of prehistoric plants and animals that have become stone (pages 14-15).

**Iron and Nickel** some of the different types of metals found in Earth (page 25).

**Larvae** a stage in insects' life after they have hatched from their eggs (pages 8-9).

**Magma** liquid rocks 700 kilometres deep (page 23).

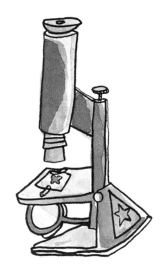

**Microscope** special magnifying lenses that can help us to see tiny things by making them look much bigger (page 2).

**Minibeasts** small creatures like insects, worms and spiders (page 7).

**Prehistoric** the name we give to long ago, before the time when people began to write history down (pages 14, 16, 17).

**Pupae** a stage in insects' life when they begin to turn from larvae into adults (page 9).

**Volcano** place in the Earth's surface where the molten rock called magma pushes its way to the surface. Volcanoes can be on land or under the sea, and they can grow into mountains or even islands (page 23).

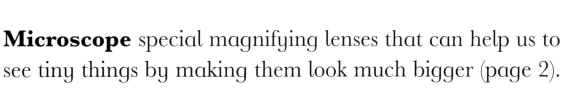

# To Paula

This edition 2004

First published by Franklin Watts
338 Euston Road, London, NW1 3BH

Franklin Watts Australia
Level 17/207, Kent Street, Sydney, NSW 2000

Text and illustrations © 1996 Mick Manning and Brita Granström
Notes and activities © 2004 Franklin Watts

The illustrations in the book were made by Brita and Mick
Find out more about Mick and Brita on www.mickandbrita.com

Series editor: Paula Borton

A CIP catalogue record for this book is available from the British Library

ISBN 978 0 7496 5685 0

Dewey classification 551.1

Printed in Singapore

Franklin Watts is a division of Hachette Children's Books, an Hachette Livre UK company.